World Class Tennis Mentality

A Player's Manual

A.J. Dowsett

1663 LIBERTY DRIVE, SUITE 200
BLOOMINGTON, INDIANA 47403
(800) 839-8640
WWW.AUTHORHOUSE.COM

© 2005 A.J. Dowsett. All Rights Reserved.

No part of this book may be reproduced, stored in a retrieval system, or transmitted by any means without the written permission of the author.

First published by AuthorHouse 09/26/05

ISBN: 1-4208-7341-5 (sc)

Printed in the United States of America
Bloomington, Indiana

This book is printed on acid-free paper.

NOTE...

This manual has been in the writing for 2+ years and is a culmination of many different seminars over the years, coupled with my experience in this field I have gathered along the way. I cannot simply even begin to tell you where from or who from for that matter I gained this information. Some exercises or pieces of information I believe came from divine inspiration literally from the bath tub to journeys on the road and the many hotels I have stayed. Hence unless stated feel free to copy, pilfer and use any part of this for yourself as you see fit to enhance not only yourself but those under your guise. The Tennis Psyche System itself is protected under copyright along with the playability scale and the goalset master plan. However, a simple email may suffice to enhance utilisation in any material you wish to write personally.

This Manual should be utilized as such exercise by exercise although you can read through first to get the idea and then back up to exercises that you feel are relevant to you.

At the end of the manual take a look at the people who I believe to have been my mentors, and whose material and work you should read at some stage or other. Regardless of whether you have heard of these names before.

Contents

Aim/Mission	1
Learn to lose correctly	3
Tennis psyche checklist	5
Goalset Master Plan - journey of a lifetime	7
Dream List – Understanding the Goalset Masterplan	10
Self-Motivation	12
How do you spend your day, Completing Goals	14
Principles of the Brain	16
More on thoughts	19
Learning to act and Listening to Self Talk	20
Changing Thoughts and the 7-Day Thought Diet	24
The Art of Concentration	27
Understanding Self Defeat - Fear, Anger	28
Anxiety, Perfectionism, Competitiveness	30
The Playability Scale	32
Why control your emotions	34
The Tennis Psyche System	36
Understanding the System	38
Relaxation - Stages 1 and 2	40
Relaxation - Stage	42
The Art of Confidence	44
Routines - Pre-Competition, 1-2 Weeks prior, The Day Before	51
The last few hours	53
Changeovers	55
More Matchplay Scenario's	57
The Finale	60
A Final word – Putting it all together	61
Athletic Psyche Schedule	64
Continuing education and suggested reading	65
Understanding your Environment	66
Tennis Tech & Tact List - Appendix II	67
Listing Your Dreams - Appendix I	69
Goalset Master Plan - Appendix III	72
Goalset Graph	73
How do you spend your day – Appendix V	74
Negative Feelings and Thoughts – Appendix VI	75

Introducing the Mission and Aim of The Tennis Psyche System

Welcome to a world of mental training, a comprehensive and simple to follow programme that includes everything you need to set you on your way to better performance.

Already you have proven to yourself that you want to improve your performance by buying into this programme. Understand that it is easy to do each and every exercise but also even easier not to!! Unless we have a great magnetic pull in committing to our future we will end up procrastinating (which is an absolute crime in my book), but do not fear this manual will teach you how to motivate yourself from within and that is huge.

Lets begin with this now age old question.........How much of your game is mentally related to your performance?

From my years of experience and of asking this question to potential top athletes I have heard replies ranging from 60% to 95%. I'm not sure you can put a figure on this! After all, how can you measure the mental performance of an athlete and what he is thinking and feeling?

A better question would be 'How much of your training time do you spend working on mental training skills compared to how much of your performance is mental?'

The answer.... Probably next to nothing, after all who can pay for £1000's for the services of a sports psychologist when the average Tennis player is trying to stay in the sport in order to earn world-ranking points, and even after obtaining sponsorship money this is always needed elsewhere, gee what a catch 22. On the other hand how can you gain world-ranking points quicker and easier without a sport specialist? This is what prompted me to write this manual.

I think it is fair to state that if you practice with purpose in the right way with the right intensity then you will be able to take a path to somewhere near to where you wish to be, we need to reach a stage whereby every part of your game is not about whether you hope you can hit a shot in a specific situation, even think you can hit it for that matter, it is better to believe you can do it, or know you can do it, but guess what, to reach the top this isn't enough you have to know you WILL do it!!!

This programme will give you everything you need to set you on your way to your end goal, along with the tools, exercises and confidence building projects, however in the meantime you should understand and utilise these principles to help you begin your journey:-

1. *To give 110% effort 100% of the time*
2. *To maintain a positive state regardless of the situation or outcome during practice or matches*
3. *To observe a no excuse mentality throughout*

You would also do well to understand the following in top class athletes

1. *An utmost desire to improve and be the best they can be*
2. *Possession of an unconditional Love of what they are doing*
3. *The ability to believe they have won before they step into the athletic arena*

To this end, what is it that we are trying to achieve?

Surely we wish to achieve our long-term dream or goal that we have set in our earlier life. In order to do this we will start our journey by understanding where we are in our present tennis life in relation to what needs to be accomplished. Of course in order to achieve our end goal (although there truly is no end) we need to play to the best of our abilities in all realms of technical/tactical physical and mental. By becoming more physically fit, maintaining efficient, effective and consistent strokes and by staying mentally in control of our mind and hence emotions this will all aid in our war of taking the edge from our opponents we play against on our own tennis tours.

With that take a good look at this:-

ATHLETIC TALENT IS THE ABSENCE OF MENTAL, PHYSICAL AND EMOTIONAL OBSTRUCTIONS.

A truer set of words have never been said!!

All 3 are closely interlinked and an imbalance in one naturally affects the other.

A quote from most aspiring Touring Players amidst obtaining world ranking points ... 'they give you nothing'. At these levels it can only take one roar of negative anger, one moment of concentration loss and that could be a foot in the door for your opponent, and a foot out for you!!

Hence further aims....

LEARN TO LOSE CORRECTLY... by
1. *Giving yourself the freedom to go for your shots and if you miss accept it pro-actively not Re-actively, learn to respond rather than react.*
2. *Recognising that with each point you have the choice to let a mistake affect you or not!*
3. *And also that the next point is more important than the last at this moment in time.*

It is of the utmost importance that you create and maintain an environment that gives your opponent the greatest potential to crack under pressure by being more physically fit, obtaining efficient consistent strokes and by staying mentally in control. At which stage you can aptly play a game I call 'allowing your opponent enough rope to hang themselves'. (In other words let them beat themselves up to make your task easier).

In the next few pages we are going to learn a great deal about ourselves, our situation and environments. We are going to find out before we start our journey where exactly we are in our tennis life and then build a bridge to where it is we want to go, whilst adding motivational exercises and thoughts to help along the way.

Now I know what you are going to say, but we have heard all this before. By God so have I!! A 100 times over but guess what, I never took this on board not once. I was one of those students who thought 'yes great heard it all before' but did I utilise it?? No, not once and why? Because every book, every lecture, every teacher gave me the facts, the what to do not the HOW TO DO!! This is why I have given you a practical guide to follow from start to finish.

Start by checking the Psyche checklist and see where you rate, anyone rating World Class email tennismentality@psycheuk.com I want to know who you are!!!

As always I now would like to Welcome you to the Beginning of your World Class Journey!!

Andy Dowsett
Director and Founder Psycheuk

Tennis Psyche Checklist

Check out the following and see where you are deficient in your Tennis Mentality.
Tick or Cross each statement accordingly:-

- ☐ I use the tennis psyche system during my performances

- ☐ I utilise, understand and evaluate a goal setting master-plan

- ☐ I have pre-match, mid-match and post-match physical and mental routines

- ☐ I monitor my thoughts/feelings and can change these to suit my current situation

- ☐ I monitor my intensity levels and adjust these accordingly before my performance

- ☐ I understand how the brain works

- ☐ I have mastered the ability to act

- ☐ My personal practice and match play closely relate to each other with purpose

- ☐ I practice my mental game daily on and off the court

- ☐ I fill out a journal daily to enhance awareness

- ☐ I monitor my game plan at various points in my matchplay using the playability scale

- ☐ I use visualization in practice and at all times throughout a match

- ☐ I am aware of my personal breathing techniques

- ☐ I have an understanding of the zone state and understand how to enhance this state

- ☐ I use positive past experiences and future memories to enhance my performances

- ☐ I take time to review my performances regardless of the outcome and note thoughts in my journal

- ☐ I have the ability to improve on my performance daily by giving 110% 100% of the time

- ☐ I utilise Psyche Intervention tools during practice and matchplay

- ☐ I maintain a balanced synergetic lifestyle

- ☐ I am self-motivated throughout my daily life

Total up the ticks and see how you got on...................

18-20   World-Class Tennis Mentality
14-18   Top-Class but lacking in areas, need to instil Tennis Psyche into your tennis programme
10-14   'Learning via the 'School of Hard Knocks'. A fun journey but time consuming.
1-10   A long way to go, welcome to the start of your world class journey!

Goal-set made Simple - The First Steps for your Journey

It amazes me that Goal Setting should be the most simplest thing in the world but yet how many people actually commit to writing down there goals? Ask yourself this and then add yourself to the long list!

I'll never forget when a good friend and mentor of mine asked me what my future goals were, I thought I was doing a good job by explaining to learn everything and become the best coach I can be and with the experience and knowledge I have now believe that still to be true (although please understand that learning is a life long journey and it never truly ends!), however this was a great mission or aim but he actually wanted to see my goals. It was not a surprise to him that I actually had none (a common occurrence among a lot of players and generally people in life!).

Answer this, How do you know how to get to your end destination if you do not know the route?

Right now you are alike a canoe in a river without any paddles being carried by the current and I'm not saying it's not a fun journey, it can be a fun journey but who knows where your heading, destination unknown!

As a young player and now coach I had been to umpteen sessions on goal setting coming away with not much else and still being were I started, a list of goals and but now idea how to go from there. I had heard all the phrases, dreams with a deadline, you have go to set those goals, a journey of a 1000 miles begins with 1 step.

Well yes, they all have there place but below is a master plan of what to do, when to do and how to do it, to which end I will let you progress onwards (please beware this can and should take a few hours)…

Stage 1 – Understanding your environment

This section is an awareness exercise (as are most of the exercises in this manual!) to find out your negative self-talk/thoughts and how others perceive you. By understanding this, you can then set yourself on the right track that will help make your performance and life more beneficial by enhancing the correct positive and fulfilling environment.

- In the table beneath (also see Appendix I) list the people that drag you down or hold you back with the statements they make, how much time you spend with these people per week and all the negative remarks that these people may make.

WHY? - In order to achieve what you want I need you to create the right environment. Go to the best Academies in the world that produce players and you will see, hear and feel the atmosphere, you can almost touch it and will get carried away with it all, you will want to work out on the court because everyone is working for themselves but yet working as a team.

You can create this environment by getting rid of those that are harmful to your future goals (however, ruthless this may seem!), or if not possible at least cut down the amount of time you spend with these particular people, if that is impossible then at least you can mentally prepare yourself and understand that at anytime these people are negative about your good self then it can rebound of from you and not have any affect.

Name/ Environment	Time Spent (Average)	Negative Remarks
Brother	3 Hours Daily	Why do you persist in something that is taking you nowhere?
Squad Mate	8 Hours Daily	I Love playing you its an easy win for me

Like most of these exercises go back over them later in the week or whenever you come across a negative situation. Awareness is a powerful and important key aspect in your growth process. Like many of these exercise they are more for you to become aware of these situations and to act accordingly.

Sometimes you cannot let go those you love but you can spend less time with them, or confront them with what they say or better still use what they say as ammunition for further motivation!

Stage 2 – Dreams List

Write down from as many of your dreams, aspirations, accomplishments you want and need in your life using the following questions on the Listing your Dreams worksheet at the back of this programme. (Appendix III).

What do I need to improve my Tennis? (Technical, Tactical, Physical, Mental) Fill out the 'Tennis Tech List – Appendix II' at the back of the manual to help.

Personal
Family
Spiritual
Financial
Things I wish to do (Include things you want to buy, see and do)

Now do something completely different…write down anything that is stopping you from reaching your end goal or goals.

Leave no stone-unturned write down absolutely everything no matter how silly you think this is, write as many things down as you can preferably in the next 15-30 minutes.

Remember this:-

'Vision without action can be a daydream although action without vision is almost a nightmare'

As with all these pearls of wisdom, they were picked up from seminars, lectures and real life and what's more, they have been tried and tested, welcome to the shortcut for your future tennis career.

Having finished this comply with the following steps (Appendix III):-

1. Review your list and mark out each statement as 1, 2, 5, or 10 Year Goals
2. Place the week or month that you will complete your 1 year goals

Further divide 3-5 of these goals into action steps via the Goalset Masterplan (Appendix IV).

These are inserted at the back of this programme, obviously print off as many as needed.

FOLLOW THE DIRECTIONS BELOW FOR HELP…

Understanding the Goalset Masterplan

Lets set a simple goal of improving consistency of a backhand drive due to lack of confidence in this area during matchplay. (Stated Goal). Follow this by writing down anything that may stand in your way.

The next step would be to set action steps in order to reach this goal, for instance:-
1. Take a 30 minute technical lesson with coach each week for 1 month
2. Spend 15 minutes per day hitting crosscourt to target in back 1/3 of court
3. Spend 15 minutes per day hitting down the line to target in back 1/3 of court
4. Hit backhands only to back court until 100 backhands have landed in this zone
5. Play a set and play out crosscourt on backhand side point is live when you change direction

Now set a reward for completing your mission, a punishment for not completing within the due date, I.E. extra 30 minutes on cross trainer in the gym.

And finally, whom you would use as a role model, to help. For me I used Thomas Muster for my Backhand, Boris Becker for my Serve, Stefan Edberg as a Second Serve and Pete Sampras as a Forehand. Volleys were my own and funnily enough my worst element of my game for a long time!

Place a potential completion date to this and a date that you would review this and finish it off with a mission statement of perhaps to possess the biggest most consistent backhand in my academy.

Now to end all this describe how this new found backhand would look and feel or even sound, close your eyes and visualise hitting the best backhands you can, use your role model if you want and follow some of the visualisation exercises later in the programme to aid this. You may even wish to pick up your racket and in slow motion swing your racket through the motions (top tip…if indoors ensure you move any objects in range!)

This then leaves the one and only step to take and that is to take action, perhaps ring up to book the lesson <u>today!</u> It is of utmost importance to get the ball rolling today (action TNT - Today not Tomorrow). Have you ever imagined a heavy roller starting its journey, slow to start with until it gathers momentum then you have it made. The hardest part is to start, to take action, with everything else in place the rest is up to you. But would I leave you at that, of course not. Lets talk motivation and inspiration.........

Stage 3 – Self-Motivation

How do you keep motivated to achieve your goals with that inner burning desire to be the best you can be, to keep up the work rate on court and in the gym?

The environment will help, those around you, your coaches, fellow peers, but at the end of the day its got to come from you, from within. Goalsetting and measuring your success will help, on the back of the goalset master plan is a graph for you to do this and measure each day how much of a certain factor you achieve. Remember all top athletes have an unconditional love and desire to achieve and become the best they can be. Without this how can you even think of breaking the top 200 in the world or the top of what you can achieve?

In my guise as counsellor and hypnotherapist, it is possible to revisit past events in your life or even performances that can bring back all the thoughts and feelings from that time to the current future, you will learn more about the brain in the next part of this course, but imagine before playing a match you utilise this as part of a pre-match routine to bring back the thoughts and feelings of the best performance of your life, and whats more this is totally possible! Of course we will also learn to clear your thoughts ready for the battle ahead and it is a battle. You can not lay down or relax for one moment, you literally have to write a 'DO NOT DISTURB' sign for all to see whilst you go about your game plan.

When you feel a little low and lack confidence this is a great exercise to visit and even revisit.

EXERCISE......
Envision 2 scenarios...
Scenario 1 – How your life would look if you do not complete your goal, how would this affect your overall dream??
Scenario 2 – How your life would look after you have completed your goal!!

AND this is the secret, always envision the negative and then the positive when you are feeling low. Eventually you will only need the second scenario to motivate yourself.

BUT Understand this, as humans we can grow to whatever we wish, you have to want to grow to your full potential, that is a profound statement so I will re-iterate this, YOU HAVE TO WANT TO GROW TO YOUR FULL POTENTIAL!!! Learn to become two things, infact you can learn by two of life's greatest workers:-

Trees - a tree will grow as big as it can given all that it has got. Can you imagine a tree suddenly turning around and thinking that's it I am growing no more, time to relax. NO! for the remainder of its life it will strive to become the best it can be.

Ants - How hard working are these little creatures. Have you ever placed an object in its way, what will it do! Find a way around, find another path, it will continue on its mission until it has been fulfilled then it will continue again. But for who? Why? For what? For the rest of the ant population.

Imagine that, setting a goal not just for yourself but for someone else! Remember Rocky 4? Rocky defeated Ivan Drago, for what, because he was fighting in his comrades name Apollo Creed! Was it for the money, NO! Something a lot more powerful, he was fighting for someone else.

How powerful to set your goals not only for yourself but to include someone else!
IS THIS MOTIVATION ENOUGH? If not, then I guess what you want is not what you really desire and I suggest you go do something else instead. Period. REMEMBER, if you wish to be in the top 200 you had better train and become better than everyone else in the world bar 199 players and that's just for starters.

How do you spend your day?

There is so much in the world that can take our focus away from what we truly want, not all contributing towards our career as a tennis player. Should we allow this? Shed the dead wood, lighten the load, and take your career more seriously. Spend your time studying the game of others, working on your own visualisation, understanding the game more instead of visualising the latest T.V. or computer programme

Complete the exercise below, this should be done for an average week, Monday to Sunday, this will show you how you spend your time. This for some of you will be an eye opener.

Write down how you spend your time including sleep, eating, (I.E. recovery exercises). Again Remember awareness is a powerful aspect and is key in development process! Use Annex V to fill this out.

Time	Activity	Comments
06.30	Wake up	10 Minute Breathing & Meditation Work
06.45	Breakfast & Shower	ETC.........

SO…is there anything here that you need to get rid off, are you getting enough recovery from the court and gym work you are doing? Are you eating enough at regular intervals?

What are you doing to recover from a hard days work? When are you doing your daily visualisation work (more on this later)?

So hopefully, you are well on your way to creating the perfect environment for your career, setting the right performance goals and working at them, don't forget to review these often and move onto finishing more on your dream list. You should have a lot to get through!

Set out your day and change it accordingly so you can accomplish the most instead of wasting time, you will then be able to reach your goals quicker. More importantly review your goals as often as possible, 1 a month at the least. (Not enough really but lets start a little realistically).

Like all of these exercises if you wish for me to review them and help you out you can email tennismentality@psycheuk.com and I will help you out, give you pointers and guide you on your way.

Now it's time to move on, email me if you have any problems. We will spend some time on looking at how the brain works and how you can use your thoughts more efficiently for performance

Completing Goals

Everytime you complete a goal first and foremost congratulate yourself, treat yourself and then look along your dream list to the next most important/pending and move onto complete that one also. This is why you must evaluate your goals regularly, certainly after you have completed one. The minute you complete a goal a whole new batch of pathways open up for you and you may feel the need to add more or take some away.

Please also understand that for every goal you write, you may realize that the action steps are more goals within themselves and these will obviously lead to yet more goals to complete leading to the main goal you need completing. Not all goals are completed in one bound, but in smaller chunks.

Principles of the Brain

Every thought you have sends electrical and chemical signals throughout your brain! Thoughts therefore have physical properties; they are real and have a significant influence on every cell in your body. For instance lets cut to the chase, think of the most erotic encounter you have had, remember this is either a past experience, something you have seen on film or something made up, either way you are using imagery to create the experience, how is your body reacting?

What just happened? Well, what you will learn in this part will affect your performance directly, by controlling your thoughts and hence your emotions you can only but improve everything about your game.

Scientific research shows that your brain can learn new things, it is just a matter of believing that you can! Even if for now you have to literally lie to yourself!

PROFOUND STATEMENTS...
Give enough focused intention to any project fully and the spirit of that project will grow and give itself back to you ten fold.

This is right up there with...
As within, so without.
The Kyballion

It took me a long time to understand either of these,
I wonder how long it will take you?

But believe me science has shown that your brain if used regularly will grow, after all you never truly grow old…if you become a lifelong student of learning. We generally either allow it to grow or we can allow our mind to literally die or wither. This is the 'use it or lose it' type scenario. This was shown when Roger Bannister broke the 4-minute mile for the first time ever closely followed by over 200 more in the following years. If you have someone in your training or match play you can spar with then this will help take you to new heights.

The trouble is, we naturally, as humans, (well for 95% of the population at least) place self-limiting chains on ourselves by allowing negative self-talk that influences what we achieve, or even worst prevent us from trying something new because we are fearful that it just will not work or it is impossible to do.

The following was learnt from a very knowledgeable Doug Bench and his Science for Success Systems (www.ScienceforSuccess.com). The reason I feel the need to tell you this is two fold. Firstly I wish for you to know the source of this geniality and Secondly if its wrong then Doug should have known better!!

So first we must understand an important experiment that took place, volunteers were asked to do simple maths problems whilst being observed under a PET scanner (computerised technology that literally scans the brain). Ideally when calculating maths problems only one certain part of the brain should light up, however whilst in the scan a fascinating and unexpected event happened……another 5 areas lit up, so each subject was thinking in 6 different areas of the brain at once!

Further studies proved that by admitting sedatives to willing volunteers, neuroscientist found that the one area calculating the problems fazed out leaving the other 5 working away. Hence the conclusion being that these 5 parts were on a non-conscious level and hence only 1 part on a conscious level. More importantly since you are unaware of your non-conscious thoughts, your non-conscious brain can'not tell the difference between what is real or imagined, truth or a lie. Hence why the phrase 'Fake it until you Make it' is all too real and should be utilised at every opportunity.

Now do the maths yourself, $1/6^{th}$ or $5/6^{th}$, where should the majority of our tennis play be??? Cut out the conscious thinking and you are on to a winner, better still cut out the conscious thinking and do enough to get inside your opponents head and you will take the upper hand which could be enough to take the match. But lets not end on that note! Take this in, the $5/6^{th}$ Non-Conscious actually thinks 10 million times quicker than the $1/6^{th}$ Conscious. Enough Said Period.

How is this for a figure......
Around 90% of our normal behaviour is based on habits, we are literally creatures of habit, your serve, return of serve and between point routines need to become a habit, this is why you need to practice purposefully and whole heartedly!

A VERY COMMON PROBLEM......
It is very easy to gain confidence in practice due to the routines and eventual mind-set this produces. However, unless your practice mirrors the intensity or preciseness of your own personal match play you will lack in confidence in your match play which for most potential athletes is a different mind-set entirely!!! You must train and practice as if it is your actual performance day.

Habits are literally rituals and rituals should bring confidence in your ability, focus and emotional control. Without rituals you are hoping for divine intervention. And to that end Good luck!

To put it another way, Imagine being in an emotionally tight situation/environment whilst battling on the court. The score is even tighter but you can find refuge in the rituals and routines that you have completed thousands of times over your playing and training career. The player with these who can bring about that extra bit of confidence in his abilities will win every time.

Back to thoughts...
Thoughts can become habits, each time you repeat a thought it is more likely to become a habit, we generally make 40,000+ thoughts a day and 60% of these are repeated daily! So if you spend most of your day thinking negatively or about what you don't want...you will only endure with the following...

Dwell on a negative thought and you are almost guaranteed a negative outcome!

IMPORTANT, IMPORTANT... You step up to the baseline at an important point on your serve you tell yourself now's the time not to double fault! Oh Dear, understand the mind is like a VCR and has stored every detail of what you see in your life, and the more you see something the more accessible it becomes. What you have done here is instruct your mind to retrieve a past memory or picture and then instruct the brain to carry out the instructions to the muscles that were encoded within this image. So hence 9 times out of 10 you will double fault...**IMPORTANT, IMPORTANT.**

Get the picture? If not you had better learn quickly! To that end I leave you with one of the best quotations I have ever come across...

Changes do not happen in a day, they happen Daily! (This is evidently a profound statement) so I best state this again...Changes do not happen in a day they happen Daily!

So, now that you are beginning to understand how the brain works, what do you do about it to help yourself perform to the best of your ability?

Most importantly is the ability to CATCH your negative thoughts, CHANGE them and COACH them to a better way. When this is completed often enough as with everything you will become very adept at this and it will become an automatic situation. Utilise these 3 C's and your game and life will improve dramatically.

So to move on and in no particular order...**THE RULES...**

1. Learn to Act

Ever heard this…'whether you think you are or think you aren't, can or can'not, will or will not you are right!!'

Jim Leohr a top Sport Psychologist in America states that you need to fake it till you make it, what does this really mean?

I believe this is working in the 5/6th part of your brain! Remember the non-conscious cannot tell the difference between what is real or imagined. Like goal setting you need to live the belief 'as if' it was, this means spend your time thinking what you do want rather than what you do not want.

EXERCISE…if you are struggling with your performance or an aspect of your game one day, act 'Like you are…'. I spent many days acting like I was Ivan Lendl throughout countless matches, this worked for me and may do the same for you!

You must act on the court at all times as if you are confident and that your opponent is not getting to you. You need a umpire type mentality, (whilst of course learning throughout), understanding that an umpire only calls what he sees and then lets it go, if the ball is out its out and he lets it go and vice versa.

Tour Players are instructed on this I am sure after all it is good to know when your opponent is handing you the match on a platter! Alternately you do not wish to show that you are handing the match to your opponent! It is of utmost important that you are in control of your thoughts in order to keep your emotions in check.

Your mindset here should be - 'I am in Control and Nothing can stop me' and for this you need a military type look in between points, give nothing away, save your energy for your match play don't literally give it away by meaningless tantrums (although a burst every now and then can at the same time be quite cleansing!). To act confidently your body language must be confident, I spent 9 years in the armed forces, chest out, shoulders back, make yourself look tall…try it, it works, and the energy exuding from this is that of pure confidence, this means you literally grow the energy from within.

Positive and Negative Actions......

Whilst on the subject of acting remember also that all negative actions are not necessarily resulting in negative outcomes and all positive actions do not always result in positive outcomes, it's what you do after these actions that make the following scenarios positive or negative. You must learn from each and every outcome and refrain from making the same mistake twice!

2. Listen to your Self-Talk

Cut out the negative in your self-talk, our everyday thoughts negatively outweigh what we think positively each day. Never finish a negative statement, never say never and never say cannot or impossible. Remember Think a negative thought and you will generally get a negative result.

BUT...How hard is it not to think Negatively? In actual fact it is very difficult for most of us, and this has been ingrained into the human Psyche since the beginning of time, in the days of dinosaural survival every noise sent out alarm bells for either food to be hunted for or to run in order not to be served as lunch. It worked then otherwise we may not be here now. The fight or flight response then was very useful but in today's age generally this becomes stored stress hormones in which we have no outlet to fight to release the influx of hormones or even to give flight in which the hormones distributed throughout the body can be used. This is then stored and over time can become unhealthily dangerous. (Best to exercise somewhat when stressed to subdue and cleanse these hormones!)

WHAT TO DO WHEN YOUR THOUGHTS TELL YOU THAT YOU ARE TIRED......
EXERCISE...Run on the spot for 1 minute and see how you feel. When you sit down and relax your body temperature drops and this sends signals to your brain that you are getting ready to relax and hence become tired, lethargic and sleepy. Scientifically, you are tired because you body has cooled down, so exercise and the body warms up and hence you feel more alert!! No excuse for not training on those tired days.
Although on that note beware of burnout.
Lethargy and burnout are two different things.

As mentioned before it's okay to think negatively but the aim is not to finish it, literally stop it in its tracks. With enough practice of doing this you can literally change the way you think, bearing in mind that our brain changes daily and can grow and create neural pathways continuously. The more we complete the same exercise the stronger these pathways become and the better we think. The better we think the more emotionally controlled we become and the more mentally stronger we become and hence the stronger the neural pathway becomes...I think you get the picture.

For all negative thinking or thoughts you find difficult to rid from your mind then you will find the next exercise very useful.

Changing Thoughts
First and Foremost I want you to think how you would like this situation or thought to be, write it down if it helps. This is your set-up for later in the exercise.

Next, find a place to relax and become aware of your breathing. Become aware of the rhythm of your breathing and perhaps the beating of your heart. Close your eyes and just R-E-L-A-X.
Now, take the situation or thought in mind and put this into a still picture, almost as if you have taken a photo of the scene yourself. Take a look at the picture and then complete the following steps...

- *Imagine where the photo is if you projected it out in front of you and change the position of where the photo is in your mind, if on the left move it to the right, if in the below move it up.*
- *Change the colour of the picture maybe to black and white, or all red*
- *Shoot the image into the distance as far as you can until it becomes a speck*
- *Send a missile speeding towards this speck and watch it disintegrate whilst....*
- *Almost at the same time another image moves towards you with the set-up situation you imagined at the beginning.*

Repeat as often as possible until you feel a change in your own feelings and reactions to what it was that is no longer troubling you.

Prior to and during matches we can cut down the amount of thinking if we are having (generally known in the trade as having a 'complete mare!'), by choosing to repeat a Mantra something like 'solid and controlled' over and over again. (Please ensure you make your own mantra though, something that will become personal for you). This works purely because it quietens the Conscious Mind or the $1/6^{th}$ of your brain.

Thoughts, The Brain and a 7-Day Thought Plan......

Let's learn more about the brain. As you now understand, your brain thinks in images or pictures. You also know that your brain can in no way tell the difference between what is real and what is imagined, whether this is negative or positive. In fact a negative phrase only brings heightened interest and awareness to the situation or thought.

Let me explain why and how. Your conscious or even the $1/6^{th}$ of your brain uses filters to stop the 40,000+ thoughts you take in every day and these are often questioned at some of the most awkward times if they conflict with your beliefs or life values, the non-conscious (the part that you utilise to play in the zone) or $5/6^{th}$ of the brain however, has no such filter and hence thoughts can be and will be utilised quicker whether negative or positive. This is why it is important to live in the non-conscious when you play matches thinking only of the shots and plays that you are to commit to.

To enhance this and become automatic at anything you do (hence creating habits) you need to create the 3 following situations:-
1. **Repetition, Repeat, Replicate, Duplicate, or do it again and again and again**
2. **An Emotional Atmosphere (Better to enjoy/love the work otherwise forget it) Evidently this is not to say that a negative environment has not created great players!**
3. **And a Motivational link to make it personal (the job in hand needs to have a motivational cause or goal behind it to make the process complete).**

Let me ask you a question…why is it that Argentina and Russia (at least on going to press), producing the most successful players to date? Check out the economy of these countries and you will understand why!! Believe me there is plenty of motivation to succeed in this respect and they will go all out to do it. Produce one role model and let the flood gates open.

However, without digressing too much…The more you send a message or thought down the same brain pathway the easier it becomes for the thought to be retrieved in the future. This without fail will take between 21-30 days for the pathway to open and fire automatically after that. Miss a day and you can expect to start all over again, for the average unmotivated person this can take 6-8 Months.

Don't think we are stopping there though…read on…

Therefore, from my opinion the brain is one of the most if not the most important tool that you should utilise in your athletic body. You should know that it too requires food to function (ideally glucose), oxygen (fact - the brain uses 25% of your oxygen intake) and water. Your brain must be hydrated to function at its highest level; in fact if your brain is slightly dehydrated this may cause a loss of up to $1/3^{rd}$ of the efficiency of your brain to access thoughts. If you are thirsty, you are already dehydrated and on your way to losing half the brains efficiency to function. After all another important fact is your brain is 90% water so for electrical impulses to flow and thoughts to be accessed or even evaluated you must stay hydrated to function at high levels. (believe me this is just the very basics but take note and heed either way!). For more information visit www.foodforperformance.com

Work out who you are and change your thinking by……

Spending the next 7-Days writing down all your negative thoughts and feelings. (Use Appendix VI for this). If you can stop yourself in your tracks so not to finish a negative sentence (or in other words change the thinking of what you don't want and converting it to what you do want) then all the better.

It is not so much of the positive thoughts that are needed but the interception of the negative. This is called cognitive therapy and has been proven that this type of therapy truly does change the brain. However, know this, all meaningful change within your brain always first starts as a falsehood, an imagination, or a visualization. This is always true before it works its way into your reality or conscious levels of your brain. How you use this extremely powerful Brain tool is very, very important!

Important Notice…Garbage in Garbage out is true!!!
But so is Good in Good out!!!

3. Stay in the Present

Why worry about the past, can you physically change it? Can you physically change mistakes on the court or situations not within your control? I say physically because mentally you learn from this and change the pictures to what you do want before letting go and moving on.

Has the future happened yet? Are you sure you are going to lose? Is it definite that your game is going down hill? You can learn from the past but not the future, do not F-E-A-R the future (Future Experiences Appearing Real), here you are merely working with the $5/6^{th}$ that will believe this is real and at the same time will go all out to make sure this becomes the norm!

So the Key? **Stay in the Present, the Moment, the Now.** By thinking about the past or future how can you possibly be concentrating on the task at hand, become mindful of what you are thinking literally.

You may have already achieved this at sometime in your playing career but guaranteed to have had this feeling elsewhere in life. By staying in the now you are already on your way to **Working or playing in the zone!** This has been achieved when you ask the following question at a stage in your life works...... "How the hell did I do that?", in which case from my experienced you truly have become masterful at your trade and when you can do this once you can achieve this again, as long as you understand the actions that got you there in the first place!

After all......What do you think about when you play well, average, or even trash?

The next time you are involved in the 'Zonal Moment' write down as much as you can about what you did prior to this, what were you thinking, what mood where you in? How relaxed were you? What was the environmental circumstances that enhanced this process? This truly is the Holy Grail for Athletes, and can be truly achievable by the many and not just the few!

4. Learn the Art of Concentration

This is literally a continuation of the prior step understanding where your focus should be at any one time in the early stages of your career will give you a greater understanding of when you are having a mare later in your performances. Remember its all down to you and only you, unless you have an opponent whom has the ability to play havoc with your thoughts! How great is that to be able to get inside your opponents head to ruin their concentration? How many sports do you know this literally happens and can result in a red card!!

Most matches when you have a weak mental ability end up with you having to beat two players, firstly YOUR SELF!!! Most players are so good at this that they needn't worry about trying to beat there opponent (the second player).

Try these simple exercises…When your game goes 'AWOL' spend a little time focusing on the writing on the ball and nothing else, or the seams, even the hairs. You have probably heard it a thousand times but spend a few times saying bounce, hit. Bounce when the ball bounces and hit when either yourself or your opponent hit's the ball. Finally, one that works well for me pick a part of your body to concentrate on, the best one - your feet! When you are not playing too well then you almost certainly are not moving to well either.

These are great exercises to do in practice as you truly become the master of your own body and actions, move from your footwork to your weight transfer your hip rotation pre-stroke set up and hip and shoulder rotation, take backs, contact points and follow through. That's not to omit your breathing process, and relaxation/intensity levels.
TOP TIP…you do not always need a court to practice and become aware of your body!! Shadow tennis at different speeds is good enough to understand all you need.

**NOW LETS LEAVE THIS BEHIND AND
MOVE ONTO ANOTHER AREA**

Understanding Self-Defeat - Whose fault is it anyway?

Here's a clue...

TAKE CHARGE FOR YOUR OWN RESPONSIBLE ACTIONS!!

Stepping onto a court for an important match (or any match for that matter) means you need to possess the ability to defeat two opponents, your actual opponent and more importantly yourself. You have no chance of defeating an opponent if you cannot control or win the battle with yourself.

This is though no mean feat, may I remind you competitive toughness is very much so an acquired skill and by no means just inherited.

To my mind and from experience working with Athletes of all sporting arenas, there are a number of reasons why players find it difficult to win the battle with themselves. Maybe it's a lack of confidence in certain skills? Or perhaps a lack of routines? Or both and perhaps even all the above!!! We shall talk about routines and confidence drops later but...IF Personal Awareness is a key to greatness read and understand the following situations...

Internal or External Distractions, Indecision or 'Scattered Energy', Fear, Anger or Anxieties. Let's look into each, the first three on the list will be dealt with via routines (the absolute cure for all winning mindsets!).

Fear – The root of all routes. Let me remind you - FEAR is a future event, So if the future is yet to exist what is there to fear? The past cannot be changed regardless of what has gone on, so lose the emotion of past events and evaluate instead. If you let go of the past and have no worry about the future this leaves what is all but important...the moment! Stay in the moment, do not fill your thoughts with experiences no longer in your control or that are yet to happen. This is a major key to playing in the zone. It is the FEAR of failure, and the FEAR of losing that hurts us, not failure.

Fear will only paralyse your performance...is that what you really want? What you really, really want!

Anger - This is born out of two experiences; expectation or frustration and either at the end of the day has FEAR as a root cause. ANSWER THE FOLLOWING QUESTIONS…"I am angry because…X", "I am X because…Y", "I am Y because…. (please continue to such time you have an 'aha' moment).

Showing your opponent that you are angry will only let them know that you are on a downwards slide of hopelessness, why give them an extra edge whilst you beat yourself up. At most levels you have taken the rope and are just about to hang yourself **(quote "give your opponent enough rope to hang themselves first" unquote),** your opponent now has an easy job to do, stay consistent and the job is done, infact hell can I play you?

Anxiety – I am anxious because...? What is the cause, certainly some image pre-empts this anxious moment. How can we help this particular obstacle? Perhaps it is the pressure of the situation, learn to love the battle on the court, love the fighting arena no matter who the opponent, remember a diamond is nothing but a lump of coal under pressure, so BECOME A LUMP OF COAL, Enjoy the pressure.

Remember though a harder more formidable opponent will challenge you and help you grow!

ULTIMATE AIM

Every time you set foot on the tennis court, whether in practice or for match play you should be prepared to work. One foot on the court means a change in attitude, this is your work arena your work place; do not take it lightly, a day less than 100% is a day lost. Add the lost days and you end up behind those who are willing to work, those willing to give all for what they believe and want.

Another Jem - YOUR ATTITUDE AFFECTS YOUR ALTITUDE
Zig Ziglar

Exercise...take one step on the court and visualise the one time in your life you worked your hardest in whatever field you can summon, grow those feelings throughout the body, brighten the images, turn up the volume of the sound and 'live the moment'. Then take the steps onwards towards a session of purposeful work. (This should already be quoted in your journal, if not why not?).

Again this needs to be practiced day in day out until eventually a foot on the court automatically triggers theses feelings and images. Oh and remember changes do not happen in a day they happen daily!!!

Perfectionism - Every shot has to be perfect right up to the technique, every match needs to be a win; every opponents winning shot is your fault! Sound familiar?

IF NOT...how about this...all your goals are unrealistic and too high for the given moment, there is a constant self critical analysis of yourself and anything you do is either good or bad, where is the middle game I ask you. Top players have a unique level they can attain when need be, and guess what? They attain this when need be, not at all times, infact I guarantee they have an ability to win when they are not playing their best tennis. They can shift up and down the gears accordingly, can you say the same?

Let me remind you - DO NOT spend time thinking about what you do not want as this will give you just that, spend your time more pro-actively thinking about what you do want. Turn the wheel and strive for perfection without attaining perfection, improve every day in every way, 1% improvement every day will send you on the way to your goal/goals. Remember tennis is not a game of perfect, but a game of striving to perform to the best of your ability in order to overcome your opponent.

Competitiveness - Over the years it has become apparent that talent is not enough to get you to the top, you also require hard work, the graft to get your there and a love for the trouble and difficulties on the way. Talent turns into a form of laziness. When you are never putting in less than you can on any given day, you are only short changing yourself, ask yourself each and everyday what did I learn about myself today, how did I improve, have I given my best effort regardless? In order of preference, I would take a grafter over talent, but a grafting talent is a different story this is a likened to a diamond amongst the coal. Above all learn to persist in all you do, setbacks should be learnt from and changed into comebacks. After all in the middle of difficulties come breakthroughs.

So, how do you play when it is all going wrong and you feel you are beating yourself and not your opponent? Check out the Playability Scale on the following page, this will ultimately be apart of your on court routines. Until such time that everything becomes routine and ultimately automatic.

The Playability Scale

This was an 'aha' moment for me one day in the bath!! How can something so simple not be utilised in a game plan, certainly at low levels however higher level players would do well to do the same when it is all going wrong! Mentality at pro level is totally different but should still be kept simple.

This scale can work at all levels from beginner to touring pro and is a guideline as to what to do in various situations, commonly found in tennis matches. A player must quickly recognise where he is on the following scale, with suggested 'positive action plans' (PAP) for each scenario:

Many Pro Players today try to play and base their games around their own particular strengths. For them this is the most comfortable way to try and win, so in essence they are in their 'comfort zone'.

The Art of Tactics is to take your opponent out of this comfort zone generally by one of Four ways:-

1. Play your game well and hopefully this will do the job
2. Change what you are doing by using changes of pace or more subtlety like varying spins
3. Playing utilizing tactical patterns or strategies using certain targets and placements on the court
4. Mentally by breaking your opponent down so that he begins to think too much

Review this only in circumstances of trouble, when playing well the art is not to think too much. With enough practice you will become automated in this area.

1-2 *Nightmare scenario, being completely outplayed or playing badly*
Two-ball survival kit e.g. serve and next ball or return and next ball. Keep looking and acting the part in order to have a chance of doing better. Clear your mind of negative thoughts using thought

changing techniques. Keep your awareness in the now, 1 point at a time by focusing on one part of your body or the ball.

3-4 **Playing *average, but not well enough to win***
Keep your emotions and body language in check, to stand a chance of moving up to the arenas of 5-8. Once again keep yourself in the now and in the job at hand by maintaining focus as above.

5-6 **Even *situation, no clear winning***
Compete with controlled ability, be aware of opportunities, and maybe take a gamble to create one. These are the matches that are won via tiebreaks and the ability to notice 'opportunity balls' and 'opportunity situations'.
If a match is consistently going to Deuce, then understand who is doing what to whom and help plan future points. (I.E. are you winning points, losing points or is your oppoenents forcing mistakes?).

7-8 ***Ahead in the match.***
Don't change a winning game - Finish the job, But be aware of tactical switch by opponent. Remember mindset should not be to protect the lead but to carry out the work that got you to this position. Remember, think in images not words.

9-10 ***Playing in the zone.***
To think too much now will place you back at worst to 7-8, make the most of it by collecting as many points as possible whilst you can.

You will have to let me know how you get on. Good visualisations and the use of anchors throughout the body can take you to a mindset of 7-10 before you even perform. This forms part of your pre-match routine that will be discussed later in the book. However poor emotional control and you can find yourself in the 1-4 area, a loss in the 5-6 of your emotions will also send you spiralling down.

Why Control your Emotions - What's the point?

Let me take you back to a time in the early days when stress levels of humans were very high. If early man's brain did not react quickly to stress the result was usually death from the physical threat of the environment around. The Fight or Flight Response was a true then as it is today.

However in today's terms, stress is not always from physical dangers but from anxiety and mental stress, yet we still have the release of those stress hormones. Our brains evolution has not caught up with our cultural evolution. When you have the release of stress hormones, physically, biologically, that makes you feel uncomfortable. And that's a good thing as it prepares you to react to the event that is about to happen.

On a slight sideline if the body has no physical reaction to these levels of stress then this leaves the stress hormones in our bodies lying dormant and stack these up over the years, resulting in any of the following……. heart attacks, strokes, asthma, even cancer…..my personal opinion and I am going to stick with it. The solution? Exercise, take a walk, run up the stairs a few times that's what our bodies were built for in the dinosaural days. Sound like Deja Vous? Good then take note.

So to that end when you feel uncomfortable and you are out of your comfort zone that is the time that you need to get really excited. If you are uncomfortable, you know that you are growing and learning something new. This is one of my prerequisites; you have to constantly learn and improve daily!

So take this to the tennis court and compare your stress levels. Stress is important to life, too little and you do not grow in fact you will only ever reach a certain level of accomplishment before hitting the wall, too much and you go nowhere from the start. What is required is a little more each time, you are under a little stress when you push a little further to your goals, reach a little higher. Play against a better opponent. Your aim is to reach higher and push further a little more each day.

Imagine playing a match and at a certain point you get wound up, but you are the quiet sort that likes to bottle things up so you keep it all under a tight lid, however more stress from the past appears and you bottle that up too, all the while your body and thoughts are more and more tense your energy is scattered along with your thoughts. Eventually the pressure builds within the bottle and something gives, generally the game and match courtesy of your thought processes. Not only are you way out of alignment with your game plan but also that which you can control, including your now out of sync routines.

One last thought and exercise to put you on the right path before moving on to help control this all important part of your body and mind and hence performance.

Exercise…Your Intensity Number
Everytime you practice or play well you are somewhere near to playing within your own personal zone and a little nearer to understanding your intensity number.

Imagine how well your body feels on a scale of 1-10, 1 being relaxed and 10 being tense, when you are playing or practicing well. Whatever this number may be I want you to write down exactly how you feel, look and think. Every little detail. Everytime you step onto the court, your work arena you are expecting yourself to prepare to go straight to the intensity zone.

The minute you walk onto the court through the gate your attitude shall change, if it doesn't then I guarantee you will not go out and practice with in a purposeful state. You need the right mindset and this is to give 110% in everything you do on the practice court as close to match play as possible.

Your aim is to achieve this, sense a change of attitude and confidence when you step one foot onto the court, if you are aiming to strive for a world ranking, do this or change your dreams, its up to you.

Now study The Crux of the whole performance 'The Tennis Psyche System'.

The Tennis Psyche System
Your between points mental game plan

Aim of Psyche System
To step up to the baseline ready for the next point, physically, emotionally, mentally ready and focused on your next objective whilst maintaining a confident ability pre-point.

Keys to Psyche System
Keys to controlling your thoughts on court is not to act while you are having self-defeating, doubting or negative thoughts. Remember your pathway after each point is either positive or a negative and its your action after the play that sets you up either way.

Psyche System in Action a step-by-step view
PLAY ENDS……..you need to **RESPOND** to one of 3 scenarios

1. Your Winner - by congratulating yourself for a job well done or understanding what set up the winner from your point of view. Replay an outstanding point again and again mentally to reimburse a good play.

2. Your opponents Winner - by understanding what produced this from your point of view or accepting a great play. Then replay this mentally the way you would have won this point.

3. Your unforced error - 'Go to the movies' by replaying a perfect point kinaesthetically or visually. (Remember this 'ANCHOR' the best and let go of the rest). Then play the perfect shot again and again.

You start the system by turning your back to your opponent and follow this with a 'Military Image' back to the baseline.

Continue with……**PREPARATION**
This is a Physical and Mental check - Relax any tense parts of the body, remember thoughts will enhance or ridicule your following point so no 'stinkin thinkin'!! (Irrational/un-useful thoughts)

Then enter into Pre-Serve or Return of Serve Routines. These are purely mental routines and not physical. Physical routines are personal but must be the same habitually throughout every serve or return of serve. Your main aim here is to lower or raise the intensity level to your given number.

Serve Routines in 5 easy steps

1. **Go to the B.A.R. (Breathe and Release)**
   This is a centering breath to relax the body and prepare it for battle
2. **Question what's my best plan of action now?**
   This helps with understanding your last play, your game plan and visualisation of the next step
3. **Step up to the Plate - (Look opponent in eye)**
   This is to happen only when (and only when) you have a clear, concise idea of your next play
4. **Visualise to Realise**
   Understand what your mind sees your body will adhere to, alternately use a feeling that brings confidence to your serve
5. **Let it rip**
   Don't wait a moment longer, go for it

Return of Serve in 5 easy steps

1. **Go to the B.A.R. (Breathe and Release)**
   Centering Breath
2. **Visualise returns of both sides**
   The server is in control so maintain the correct mindset 'this ball is going back'
3. **Step up to the Plate - (look opponent in the eye)**
   Mentally re-emphasise this ball is going back
4. **Look for clues on serve early on**
   Scouting will help this but if not try to pick up cues early in the set
5. **Trained Instinctive Response**
   This is from hours of practice, self-doubt is of no use now, go for it

Understanding the System

By now you understand that we play differently under pressure purely because the stress of competition literally causes our body and thoughts to change (as discussed earlier), but with the correct purposeful training, there is no reason why you cannot enhance your competitive play. The tennis psyche system will give you the ability to play in an environment that you have practiced in for years.

Also understand this...when used often enough and you enter the ZONE, you will be unaware that the above is happening you enter a realm that everything has slowed down, the ball looks the size of a basketball and you even seem to predict plays before they even happen. Enter this once and you will have opened a gateway to continue this again and again, IF, and only IF you remember what you did to get you there in the first place, you need the same feelings, thoughts, routines and a near similar environment to help facilitate this. That's why you must write it down in your journal.

Keep a Journal...
A journal is a simple book where you write down your thoughts and feelings throughout your day, from practice to matches. You will write down anything that comes to mind and perhaps anything that will be required for your ultimate dream. Why not start by noting how you physically run through a service routine I.E. how many steps do you take past the baseline, or better still where do you like to stand pre-point? How many ball bounces do you take prior to serving? This can be your first Journal entry. Remember self-awareness is the ultimate key to greatness.

So What Does it Look Like in Action?
Okay Imagine this...you are playing an opponent you have yet to beat (actually do this now, think of someone and see yourself standing on the opposite side of the court), standing just behind the baseline you take a deep relaxing breath in and decide on the next play, (this is your choice of play but whatever it is, live in the moment). With your mind set you are ready to 'step up to the plate', (imagine this now, feelings of confidence flowing throughout your body almost into your racket). Visualise how

your racket will contact the ball and how the ball will fly and land on your opponents side of the court (if confident enough visualise the following shot or placement of next shot). Another breath or final image, another full visualisation or the mention of a trigger word and then let it rip................ you receive a weak reply that you finish off for a winner in style.

Congratulate yourself with a fist pump for a great play, turn your back to the opponent and maintain a military style image past the baseline. Go through a body check for tension and mind check for negative thoughts, simply tighten tense muscles a few times and vanquish negative thoughts with the thought changing technique.

Restart the next point by going to the B.A.R!!!

With routines like this tennis will be a breeze until you meet your match and then this will be of utmost importance!!!! At this stage it will be the player who can control their nerve that will win through. But remember this is what you absolutely relinquish, the chance to grow and build on your game.

I have placed this in now purely so that you can practice enough of this in order to implement into your Tennis Performance. And guess what... you do not need to play against anyone in order to practice this particular system!! No excuses get out there and practice.

RELAXATION TECHNIQUES

There are a number of reasons that you would need relaxation techniques….and any/all of the following apply

To Aid Visualisation work and Self Hypnosis Techniques
To help lower the heart rate between points in preparation for the following play
For enhancement of general relaxation in order to regain energy from a heavy duty day

The First Stage in relaxation techniques is the ability to breathe in the correct way, do not move on to the following stages until this has been accomplished. We touched on it earlier but there is no harm to do this again.

> *Sit or Lie down in a comfortable position and take one long slow deep breath through the nose filling air into the stomach first, count how long it takes to do this comfortably (i.e. 7).*
> *Hold the breath comfortably for up to twice the amount counted in (i.e. 14).*
> *Breath out through the mouth as much air as possible slowly by pulling in the stomach area whilst thinking of a relaxing image, or phrase (i.e. relax), or even using a feeling within the body.*
> *Then spend as long as possible attempting to think of nothing, every time a thought enters let it pass and retain a non-thinking moment.*
> *Continue twice daily without fail for as long as possible.*
> **Evidently, the non-thinking is crucial for pre-match routines!!!**

The Second Stage carries on from the above whereby eventually a few deep centering breaths will enhance relaxation within the body and mind. Which can obviously be utilised on the court!!

Now, onto this particular exercise, it is entirely up to you whether you work from the head down or the feet up but either way we are going to relax each and every part of the body in a number of ways…

Work from the toes and you can either imagine a colour, feeling (whether tingly, hot or cold) or you can tense each part in succession, spend a few minutes on each area to begin with. From the toes work to the feet, shins and calf's, around the knees and up along the legs to the hips. However, you imagine this working is your own individual way, whether spiralling throughout if visualising a colour or rising slowly if utilising feeling.
From the hips around the stomach and lower back up the spine and towards the chest, filling to the shoulders down each arm to the elbows along down to the wrists and into the fingers.
From the shoulders to the neck and upwards to the head. Imagine or feel every muscle fibre and vessel throughout the body relax and become calm, live in this moment in the way you can, perhaps a certain feeling or colour is apparent in a certain part of the body, take a note of this here (_____),
as we can use this again in a performance routine later.
When you are ready and not before become aware of your breathing and surroundings and re-open your eyes if need be, knowing that anytime you complete this cycle it will become easier, simpler, quicker and more powerful!

Task – Try out different ways to relax the whole body from head to toe or toe to head.

The Third Stage once you have easily accomplished the above next comes the ability to visualise your performance. All successful top athletes use visualisation for performance enhancement. This truly is the difference that makes a difference! But guess what like a lot of exercises its easier not to do than it is to do.

> *Take yourself to a place where you feel safe, a place where only you can be on your own, away from anywhere and everyone, a place where you are totally relaxed. This could be a room, or a particular part of the world, for me it's a beach and a whole world around it to explore. Take a good look around, view the scenery, listen to the sounds and begin to feel your own particular feelings. Take in this feelings of safety and confidence, a place where you can grow your energy and abilities throughout yourself.*
> *When you have grown this to the maximum throughout your body and beyond, now is the time to take yourself to your athletic arena and see yourself play the best you can against whomever you wish, either the top player in your County, Country or event the World!!*
> *Everything you do is perfect, your strengths grow stronger and you have no weaknesses. This is your true potential and an ability that you can take to the court.*
> *Play a few games or even a whole set whilst seeing yourself become stronger and quicker, more consistent and aggressive. Play to your hearts content until you are ready to finish whereby you can re-enter your own private safe place. This is your sanctuary away from the outside world when everything gets too much during life or match play, a place where you can visit to refocus on changeovers if need be a place to regain confidence and energy and only you can do that here.*
> *Become aware of you breathing and surroundings and slowly come back to the room.*

The more visualisation work you do the better, try and use all the senses as much as possible, visualise your best performances everyday for at least 15-45 minutes per day. The more the better and whilst we are at it follow this with a journal entry.

Studies have shown that athletes who purely practice do a great job, those that purely visualise also do just as well! BUT those who do both come out tops at all times. This is a major tool in reaching the top of the tree in your field, however understand that when you physically play do not become worried about technique, just the actual tactical play and a rough action of the set plays you wish to accomplish, work with this exuding energy and confidence that you can see throughout your body.

VISUALISE TO REALISE

Another great phrase I picked up on the way.

The Art of Confidence

Confidence is a delicate form, it can take time to build but only a second to lose!!

Self-Confidence with any athlete is important and so I will dedicate a few pages to this all important chapter and follow this with a chapter on situations within the game that are possible areas to be aware of.

If you are with Confidence then you have a strong belief in that area, with a strong belief in that area comes a great amount of energy with it. There are generally two types within this area for athletes, general confidence of own skills and specific confidence of particular skills. For instance Ali had one of the best general self-confidence abilities in the world by consistently stating 'I AM THE GREATEST'.

Exercise...state a truth about your strengths in your game, and live it. Start with I AM…

Simple enough and if you give energy and act as if it is true and you will begin to believe this too.

Specific confidence is the ability to stand up and hit a particular serve to a certain place without fail. You are confident it will work.

I believe there are 5 great confidence phrases you should ask yourself when looking at all aspects of your play…(Appendix II)

I. *I hope I can hit this shot (or perhaps you can pray for divine intervention instead)*
II. *I think I can hit this shot (this is just Stinkin' Thinkin' and it will not hold up)*
III. *I believe I can hit this shot (A great starting place but still requires work)*
IV. *I Know I can hit this shot (A great aspect but there is better to come, seek and you shall find!)*
V. *I will hit this shot (The mark of World Class Athletes)*

You should have already filled out the Tennis Tech List earlier in the Goalset Masterplan, I want you now to go back and revisit this exercise by using the scoring system above. For each shot or tactic use the following scoring system :-

I-1/2   II-3/4   III-5/6   IV-7/8   V-9/10

Confidence starts on the practice court whereby you put in 110% 100% of the time purposefully. You are required to have a belief in yourself that is unbreakable, Roger Federer believes he is the best in the world right now and who is to fault this belief!! Confidence can also be attained from what others say to you, but be careful they can also crush your confidence too!! Past performances can also improve confidence, after all winning ways breed winning ways. Become aware of new levels you attain and hold onto that rung of the ladder, don't allow anyone to knock you off. (Remember the Negative People, Places and Things Exercise?? Everything in this manual is for a specific reason otherwise its not worth reading).

Exercise…Write down a list of your strengths that you are confident with, ask fellow players or coaches that know you to state your strengths for you and compare the two. This is you , this is your game and this is the framework that has got you to where you are today (wherever that may be).

<u>**TOP TIP**</u> - *An even better question here is if I was playing against me how would I beat me??*

I have heard time and time again a coach has taken a player to the top by making them aware of there own strengths and creating a belief, a self-confidence around this. You can do this yourself…

Now we are to continue on our final exercises in this particular section **THE CONFIDENCE SCRIPT.**

This may be used as part of a pre-match routine.

At this stage it may seem like information is all over the place, do not fret this will be put into an orderly sense at the back, right now read the chapters, learn the lessons, complete the exercises and all will be well.

Exercise...Imagine a time when you played the worst match you have ever played. Put this into a still picture or if you find this difficult a moving film.

Describe the scene, write it down, colours, sounds, feelings absolutely everything, describe how you look compared to your opponent are you bigger or smaller, who looks more confident, write down everything spend some time on this.

Now put that to one side and complete the same for the best performance you have ever had the joy of playing in.

Compare the results, and notice the difference, your confidence script will derive from the best performance and will change accordingly when you improve your performances. You should notice at its very basic one picture is dull and the other bright, one lifeless and the other full of energy. More importantly what was your self talk, how were you thinking? Explore the remainder of the differences yourself, personal awareness is key!

Meanwhile, The next section gives you a few tips in dealing with potential attempts to take the confidence from you...enjoy and learn

INTERESTING SCENARIOS

The following is a list that you may have already experienced or are about to encounter

- A Feeling of not being good enough
- Nervousness before or during matches
- Practicing well but playing trash
- Negative thoughts of any type
- Intimidation by Opponents
- All problems relating to a root cause of fear
- Worrying about the anything not in your control
- Dislike of competing at particular tournaments or against particular players
- Certain environmental or situational pressures

A lot of this has already been spoken about and can be helped with steps within this manual earlier or are about to be dealt with in the remaining pages. However, the following scenarios are all too common and hence worth a mention…

Practicing Great but Matchplay is trash

The chances are you are not in control of you body or mind and are failing to stick to set routines.

Practices and matches should be Routine and Ritual based from Serve to Return of Serve and everything in between. This is what the Tennis Psyche System was invented for!

Perhaps there is every chance that you are not practicing the way you are playing, if you want tips on this then you can email your practice plan and what you do and I will give you tips accordingly. Free of Charge as part of the course.

IMPORTANT TIP…*But understand that there are also two types of self-confidence areas appearing here, you can gain great practice self-confidence and lack competitive self-confidence. Some players at certain levels just wish to play matches as practice, which is not a bad idea if that is what brings about your world class belief in yourself…* **IMPORTANT TIP.**

Exercise...Try and figure out what it is that brings about a downfall in your self-confidence, figure out where it comes from, and face the fear! (to coin a phrase). You will realise that some of these confidence slumps are within your control and others are not. Within your control can be dealt with and reframed to a more positive perspective, write down what has caused the downfall and brainstorm how to deal with this. Use the thought record Appendix VI to help.

If the fear is from match play opponents or the match itself utilise the following...

3 TOP TIPS

- Place the match in a better light
  If you are achieving another level by playing a better opponent love the battle that will help you grow. Who cares what you look like or what people will say if you lose, what are you doing looking to the future anyhow? If you are thinking like this...is it going to be the end of the world or will you live to play another day? Obviously if you are having to constantly think this way then we have to look elsewhere to enhance your mental strength. If you gain one or two extra games from your opponent than the time before then you have taken another great leap in your tennis development.

- Have you ever thought of your Opponents Perspective?
  Your opponent goes into the match possibly fearing your strengths, fearing what he is to expect. Understand though, at the same time most opponents however have dealt with this area, move on and do the same.

- Build yourself up by changing your pictures
  Remember what you have worked towards, where you have been and what you have accomplished. Utilise imagery if you fear your opponent. Grow yourself bigger and turn your opponent into a cartoon character. The sillier the better.

It's better to lose having gone for all your shots without a fear of failure than to have lost pushing, hacking and cowering your way through.

A Note on Mental Strength
Mental Strength either wins matches OR Determines the outcome!

To my mind Mental Strength is the ability to stay focused on every point throughout the match through the use of the Tennis Psyche System. You shouldn't feel mentally drained at the end of a match unless it was a grueling tight 5 setter. By using your routines and using energy strategies throughout you will finish the match in an upbeat manner mentally for the next upcoming match.

Certain areas that require your close attention in regard to focus lapses…

Closing stages of sets or matches

Beginning of sets when you won the last

Blown break point opportunities

Lost games you could/should have won

Bad calls from opponents or umpires

When you are not playing well…
A great player can still win when not playing well. Top players play so much they are rarely at their peak for most of their games.

Don't panic chances are you may be able to play yourself back in! Remember abusing yourself gives your opponent a Psychological lift.

Playing Higher Ranked Opponents…
Be aware of playing against reputation and not the opponent.

Points to note/Bear in mind
- Some opponents have an expectation to win, use this to your advantage
- Play down mind Picture reputation created by yourself

- These players are used to quick easy leads. Stick with them as long as it takes them to become frustrated.
- Go into the match knowing you can win and dig in to give all you can (Mark of a World Class Athlete)

Remember you play the ball not the opponent!
A ball knows nothing of rankings or player levels!

BACK TO ROUTINES

Become a Slave to Routine!!

Imagine if every time when it mattered you could enter a place where you were confident, trusted your abilities to the letter, focused and calm ready to do what it is you set out to do. No matter what is happening in the world around you, there could be a war going on in the next court but you are about to start your routine and nothing can deflect you from this.

Not an impossible task if you have routines to follow from point to point, changeover to changeover.

Every player has a set of routines they follow to mentally prepare themselves helping to either pump themselves up or calm themselves down. Whatever they do regardless, the main aim of routines is to have a set of habits or procedures that will instil the utmost confidence in your abilities as a player.

Lets start with the **PRE-COMPETITION** procedures

Below is a bullet point list, of what you may do prior to and running up to competition. Understand that these are personal to every individual, what works for the World Number One doesn't mean the same will work for you. But do not worry or fret we will give you a programme to work this out.

Have a look at this first…

1-2 Weeks Prior
1. **Ensure your competitive conditions are as close to your match conditions as possible**
    Preferably playing the same surface as you are going to play on, and if known find out who your opponent is in the first round and try to practice the way you would beat them.
2. **Prepare yourself with visualisation**
    This should be run of the mill by now and should be built up to 45-minutes worth of work each day/night. Try to visualise the arena you will be playing to a tee. Don't forget to visualise what may go wrong and how you would pro-actively respond to it. Everything you do here is with a positive outcome regardless.
3. **Practice for Confidence**
    This is something that works for you. Anything that gives you ultimate confidence. For me it was just serving, returning and hitting to failure, for a few hours, my partner nor myself could go to win the point just remain consistent. Then I would play 5 sets in the afternoon regardless of the score.

The Day Before
1. **Remember what you have accomplished to get here and go with what you got**
    Your periodisation plan has taken you to where you are, if you feel unprepared then you need to look at your work prior to this tournament. Remember your own strengths and what you are going to bring to the game. In the words of Pete Sampras - 'Remember who you are and where you have come from'. You should by now have a personal philosophy to instill confidence deep within yourself.
2. **Eat and Sleep well**
    There should be no excuse for not having prepared your body ready for the days task ahead. Enough said on this! Do not succumb to being a party animal you should instead be busy...
3. **Visualising the perfect game you are to play the following day**
    This is your game at your best, nothing can go wrong and this is how you will play the following day.
4. **Check your equipment**
    Check all that is applicable to you for the playing arena, from your bag to a change of shirt, maybe even a lucky shirt, have you ever noticed how Tiger Woods always wears a red shirt on the last day of a championship?

The Last Few Hours

1. On Court workout related to match play tactics

This is all for you to get your game warmed up and everything working prior to match play, I personally prefer to do this at least 2 hours beforehand….

My Particular on court workout included the following……
10 minute Service Box Warm-up
10 Minutes of Cross Court Rallying both sides
10 Minute Volley workout with Occasional Smashes
10 Minute Serve workout
10 Minute Return of Serve workout (partner serving from service line)
10 Minute point playing (longer if possible) relating to specific match play tactics

2. Prepare your Body

This is for a final routine to prepare your body for battle. For me I preferred a simple Yoga workout which stretched the whole of the body. This was called a 'salutation to the sun' and no doubt can be found on any search engine or yoga book.

3. Motivational Mental Time

This is your own time to do as you will things that will pump you up if required or calm you down. Anything to prepare you for your up and coming match. For me I had my favourite music that I played whilst visualising my perfect play. This is where you will visualize all your best shots ever played from the past matches. Every perfect serve, return of serve, volley and groundstrokes. String points together that you remember from the past that are the best plays you have ever made. This will help enter you into the zone.

4. Dress in your battle armor

Time is upon us and now at this stage you may wish to take a shower. This can be symbolic to refresh the body and take all any last remnants of negativity from the mind, washed away down the plug hole. Then dress as if you are placing your battle armor on, each piece of clothing takes you to your intensity level required to win your game.

NOW LET THE GAMES BEGIN……

The whole match will revolve around the Tennis Psyche System, a system that you have by now practiced previously.

<u>REMEMBER THE RULES ON PRACTICE</u>
Changes don't happen in a day they happen daily!
In fact I truly believe it takes 21-28 days of daily practice to place a new technique in to match play, miss a day and you may as well start again!!!
For the average player you can kiss this formula goodbye and instead take 6-9 months instead.
Your choice, either my way or the highway.

The next time you play a practice match I want you to add a scenario to it, perhaps it is the first of 4 matches you need to reach the qualifying stages of a match. Follow this on until you qualify for a tournament and then play each match in turn until you finally get knocked out. Try the whole exercise again on preceding matches and try to get further each and every time.

So with Pre-Match and Between Point Routines covered how about….

Changeovers

The 'Sanctuary' where you sit is sacred. Your place only to do as you please. Follow a specific routine suitable for you and stick with it on each and every point.

Here is an example of a good mate of mine, who interestingly used to hit with Ivan Lendl whilst still at number 1 in the world.

Walk over to seat and place racket on bag
Blow nose regardless
Towel down
Take a couple of mouthfuls of water
Control Breathing with Centreing breaths
Quick review of situation and future tactics
Another mouthful of water
Final confidence visualisation or words
And…
Walk confidently with a Military Style look to the baseline and back to the 'Tennis Psyche System'

Nothing special but I have highlighted in bold the main points. Please take note!!!

Now whilst controlling your breathing I want you to also enter what I call the energy cylinder. (This is an imaginary area around your seating area).

> ### THE ENERGY CYLINDER
> *First you need to practice this off-court. If it helps place a hoop on the floor whereby you can stand, if not imagine a circle big enough for you to stand in. Before stepping into the circle, imagine a circular wall extending upwards as far as you can imagine, touching a world unknown to you and I. The cylinder may have a colourful glow within and perhaps even a noise or buzz.*
>
> *When you are ready step into the cylinder and feel yourself becoming alive and energised, an energy melting into your body from top to toe, pulsing throughout energising you, calming you and instilling confidence throughout.*
>
> *And now you know every time you step or sit in your energy cylinder you will be revived, energised and confident to continue on your way through the next play.*

Dia Emergencies when you cannot clear your mind at any stage...

Go straight to a mantra, when used often enough your focus will become narrower and this will literally trigger your emotions back to a state you have experienced before. Once again beware this takes practice.

MORE MATCHPLAY SCENARIOS......

The following are situations in a match that are cause for thought, Literally! At some stage or another throughout this manual we have covered all eventual on-court possibilities, however if you adhere to the tennis psyche system from start to finish then there should be nothing to worry about! However, take a note of what to do when...

Finishing a Lead...A huge error athletes make when performing well or leading in a match is to become too protective of a lead. As soon as you realise that you are playing well, some players change from a mindset of playing offensively to playing defensively. The playability scale will help you understand were you are whilst playing a match if need be whilst understanding the different scenarios and mind sets required within these scenarios.

When focused on holding onto a lead, you create a mental obstacle that forces you to perform defensively. In this mindset, you focus on how to avoid mistakes instead of continuing on the same route that got you to where you are in the first place.

You get a lead on your opponent and sometimes let up or coast, or expect the win, and that's when you lose the next game, set and possibly eventual match. For many players, playing with a lead is the toughest. Others prefer this mindset, and others prefer still to play from behind. This isn't the only sport this happens, understand this can happen in Football to teams like West Ham whereby they lose the lead in the dying seconds/minutes, or when golfers lose the lead on the final few holes. (Okay I am a life long West Ham supporter why else mention the Irons?).

Without digressing to much, to remain in a leading position, you must continue to play the same game that got you there and finish the job in hand. The same idea holds true when you have momentum in a match, continue the same and build as many points as possible, whilst being on the look out for changes in momentum. You have to think, act and play the same. Don't change a thing. I teach players to imagine an animal or piece of machinery, one player used a steam roller and imagine rolling on through until the last ball was played and the ultimate words of Game, Set and Match were called.

Keep the momentum on your side. This can disappear quicker than it appeared when you start to think ahead of the present moment. When you have momentum in tennis, you have confidence and should take full advantage of it, act with confidence, stay with the on court Psyche System to the tee and you will remain in the present.

The Ability to Act

Armed with this understanding of how the mind works and of the above technique, we can turn to changing the way we think to our advantage. Take a look at the diagram below…

> **Our Environment/Situation**
> Creates our
> **Beliefs**
> In Turn Creating
> **Thought Patterns**
> That Produce
> **Feelings**
> Which Determine our
> **Behaviour**
> And the way we physically look whilst in turn Reinforcing our
> **Belief**
> And enhancing the whole process again and again.

Interesting isn't it. However if this is no interest to you whatsoever, you can forget about it, bearing in mind though whatever happens you will create this cycle of events in all that you do. Look at it like this, you are responsible for what happens on court and your reactions to any and every situation throughout your match. If you decide to get down at anytime throughout you are just running a 'must get down on myself programme' throughout your body and mind. If you decide that you are playing confidently, you are merely running a 'I am confident in what I am doing right now' programme and as is true to life your body adheres to your thoughts.

To test this try this exercise…

> *What does your body look like when you are feeling confident, what are you thinking at this time? Evidently make this a Journal time!!*
>
> *Physically how do the following parts of your body look or feel to you?*
> - *Head*
> - *Shoulders*
> - *The way one walks or carries oneself*
> - *Face*
> - *Eyes*
> - *Breathing*
>
> *Questions*
> *Which do you prefer?*
> *Which do you think works better at a higher level of performance?*
> *Is there anything you can do to bring out confidence?*
> *What are the reasons for not looking confident?*

You should also know that Life is pretty much the same, run a depression programme and you will become depressed, run a lonely programme you will be lonely etc.... and now you get the picture. Sometimes though some people relish being in the depressed state.

Finally....THE FINALE
What to do after the match.

I believe in a 24 hour rule, regardless of the outcome you have to learn from it and move on within 24 hours. If you won, review the match and write down the points of your game you could have been more efficient. Then write down your strengths. Negative before the positive.

If you lost do the same, its far to easy to think I won and not review a thing, on the other hand it is also to easy to lose and lose interest in what happened.

Some athletes go straight to the practice court after a match and work on the weaknesses when they have reviewed matches, this may work for you. Or if unable to visualise how the match should have gone. Review the film of your brain and rewrite the script. End on a positive.

TRUE STORY...I never forget when I was younger playing a match and double faulting 15 times in one set, I still eventually won, but it was the ensuing conversation that is of interest here.

The guy I played stated to me that if I had double faulted less I would have won easier!! I stated I never double faulted, after a lengthy discussion and a tantrum from my opponent stating I was mad in the head and obviously unaware of what I was doing he stormed off. To my mind and in my mind there were no double faults, never have been and never will be. (Psyche System in Action).

As a future issue I have a strong belief that I will only ever double fault once in a match if at all and to this day I am rarely wrong! (Remember act as if it is true and you will travel to horizons you have never been).

A Final Word - Putting it all Together

Before I finish and wrap up this outstanding manual and journey I will leave you with another very powerful exercise. It's all to easy for a player to become injured and do nothing whatsoever towards their own personal tennis development.

When you are injured that is the time to go full time into tennis visualization this has been discussed before and I will say it again, practice alone is not enough, the art of visualising is all too important in conjunction with your training. Both on and off court, ever realised that you play your best tennis when you merely think in pictures and nothing else, you see the perfect shot seconds before you hit your shots and end with the same execution.

To enhance your own visualisation techniques to a world class level I am working on a new manual entitled 'World Class Visualisation Techniques'. Keep an eye out for it on www.psycheuk.com for more information.

However, try this simple exercise on healing the body the crazier the images the better....

Self-Hypnotic Healing

Become aware of your breathing to help focus the mind and relax the body, (another great time to work on the non-thinking exercise!).

Now close your eyes and imagine you are at a part of your body that is injured. Have a good look at the injury and describe it to yourself.

Regardless of what it looks like and how it looks, this injury can be healed. So I want you to imagine a box by your side, a box whereby you can reach in and obtain any tool or implement available, anything you need no matter how silly this may seem, for instance if you have a big gash take a needle and thread, perhaps the area needs washing with a steam cleaner, or even glued back together.

For example - on suffering from a huge migraine one day, I completed the exercise above and utilised a chisel and hammer to take away a moulded gunge, followed by a steam clean around the brain! 15 minutes later I had just realised my migraine had completely disappeared!

Once this has been completed to satisfaction become aware of your breathing understanding that this will need to be completed every day a bit like a doctors prescription for healing to start to take place. This is very powerful use fully!!

This will take you another step forwards so let me know how everything is going.

As with all exercises and dependant on the injury, make sure you complete this exercise daily.

So where are we at? (other than at the end!)...let us review your journey.

Chances are you have read this through for all the information and have yet to put it all into practice.

Well done for reaching this far, now go back and complete the Psyche Checklist, this should show you where you are right now with your tennis mentality.

Following this if you haven't done so already complete the Goalset Masterplan to enhance your ambitions, this will bridge the way to your dreams and future ambitions. Along the way you have planned your days and worked on the environment and taken a look at your thoughts.

Reading through this manual has taught you how you personally think and how the brain works, very useful throughout your playing career.

Throughout has also touched on different scenarios that you will clamber across throughout your playing career however utilisation of THE TENNIS PSYCHE SYSTEM, will sort this out, along with the routines you have learnt along side this.

We have touched on visualisation techniques and relaxation techniques, another all too important aspect for athletes.

We have also spoken about confidence and how to instil this within yourself.

If this seems too much for you to handle alone then you can try the Eight-Week Performance Programme
listed below via phone and email.

The aim of the programme at the end is for you the Athlete to be able to play only utilizing pictures and feelings. You will have an understanding of what brings you to the zone, and how you can mentally stay there with the processes you have become now automatic.

Schedule

Week 1 –   Assessment and Relaxation Techniques

Week 2 -   The Goalset Masterplan

Week 3 -   Understanding how the brain works during performance, Controlling your Emotions and The 7-Day Mental Plan

Week 4 -   Performance Routines and your Athletic Psyche Plan

Week 5 -   A look at Outside Influences and final Assessment with ongoing Support at £5 per month.
(If Required)

For more information on this visit
http://www.psycheuk.com/Personal_Sport_Psychologist.htm

So there we have it a personalised plan for your Tennis Mentality. A course in personal awareness and an enhancement towards your athletic development.

Any problems feel free to email me and I will in turn do my absolute utmost to answer every email that ventures into my inbox.

Until then enjoy the journey, enjoy the trip, do everything you can to enhance your performance, and remember become aware every time you reach a new rung on the ladder to the top as you have raised the bar a little more. More importantly remember to have fun along the way as this path should never be a chore.

ONE LAST THING…

WELCOME TO THE BEGINNING OF YOUR WORD CLASS JOURNEY!

Continuing Education and Suggested Reading

To grow and help the world grow with you I request one thing of you, and that is to become a student of life and a teacher to others. Just by adhering to good life principles you are a role model and teacher to others. I have said this before and I will say it again, you only truly grow old when you stop learning whether you are 16 or 106, become a student of life and you will always feel young and your brain will continually grow.

The following is a list of those I have learnt from and believe are intricate in their abilities to teach and touch the Human Race. In no particular order

Paul Mckenna – www.paulmckenna.com
Richard Bach – www.richardbach.com
Jim Rohn – www.jimrohn.com
Doug Bench – www.scienceforsuccess.com
Jim Leohr – www.ptrtennis.org
James Redfield – www.celestinevision.com
Jure Biechonski – www.sachinternational.com
Dr. Bryce Young – www.ptrtennis.org
Zig Ziglar – www.zigziglar.com
Andy Dowsett – www.psycheuk.com

Buy their books, visit their websites and learn from them all.

To order a book of tables please visit www.psycheuk.com for details. This book will include all the following tables in this manual for you in an A4 size for your ease with plenty to spare.
Alternately photo copy your own!!

Understanding your Environment – Appendix I

Name/Environment	Time Spent	Negative Remarks

Tennis Tech and Tact List - Appendix II

In the columns rate yourself from 10 according to 'The Art of Confidence' Page 44. Then have your coach/playing mate rate your shots, add both scores together and divide this by 2. Follow this by taking an extra point off for motivational, character building purposes.

	Serve	Wide Serve All Views	Body Serve All Views	Middle Serve All Views
1.	First serve flat			
2.	First serve slice			
3.	First serve topspin			
4.	First serve reverse slice			
5.	Second serve slice			
6.	Second serve topspin			

	Stroke Play	Your View	Coach View	New View
1.	Forehand crosscourt			
2.	Forehand down the line			
3.	Inside out Forehand			
4.	Off Forehand			
5.	Backhand crosscourt			
6.	Backhand down the line			
7.	Off Backhand			
8.	Backhand Slice			
9.	Forehand Slice			
10.	Forehand Lob			
11.	Backhand Lob			
12.	Forehand drop shot			
13.	Backhand drop shot			

	Midcourt Play	Your View	Coach View	New View
1.	Forehand approach crosscourt			
2.	Backhand approach crosscourt			
3.	Forehand approach shot down the line			
4.	Backhand approach shot down the line			
5.	Attacking Mid court ball above net			
6.	Mid court ball below net			
7.	Forehand Drive Volley/Approach Volley			
8.	Backhand Drive Volley/Approach Volley			

	Net Play			
1.	Forehand volley crosscourt			
2.	Forehand volley down the line			
3.	Backhand volley crosscourt			
4.	Backhand volley down the line			
5.	Forehand Touch Volley			
6.	Backhand Touch Volley			
7.	Smash			
8.	Backhand Smash			

	Return of Serve – Deuce/Ad	Your View	Coach View	New View
1.	Attacking			
2.	Middle			
3.	Body			
4.	Wide			

	Style of Play			
1.	Serve & volley			
2.	Aggressive Baseliner			
3.	Aggressive Allcourt			
4.	Defensive Baseline			
5.	Chip and Charge			

Listing your Dreams - Appendix III

Goals/Dreams/Aspirations/Ambitions/Wants	Years	Months
1.		
2.		
3.		
4.		
5.		
6.		
7.		
8.		
9.		
10.		
11.		
12.		
13.		
14.		
15.		
16.		
17.		
18.		
19.		
20.		
21.		
22.		
23.		
24.		
25.		
26.		
27.		
28.		
29.		
30.		
31.		
32.		
33.		
34.		

Goals/Dreams/Aspirations/Ambitions/Wants	Years	Months
35.		
36.		
37.		
38.		
39.		
40.		
41.		
42.		
43.		
44.		
45.		
46.		
47.		
48.		
49.		
50.		
51.		
52.		
53.		
54.		
55.		
56.		
57.		
58.		
59.		
60.		
61.		
62.		
63.		
64.		
65.		
66.		
67.		
68.		
69.		
70.		

Goals/Dreams/Aspirations/Ambitions/Wants	Years	Months
71.		
72.		
73.		
74.		
75.		
76.		
77.		
78.		
79.		
80.		
81.		
82.		
83.		
84.		
85.		
86.		
87.		
88.		
89.		
90.		
91.		
92.		
93.		
94.		
95.		
96.		
97.		
98.		
99.		
100.		

Goalset Master Plan - Appendix IV

Goal ....
....

What is preventing you from achieving this goal?

Action Steps (Process Goals)

1..

2..

3..

4..

5..

Reward	
Punishment	
Role Models	

Potential Completion Date ....

Potential Date to be Reviewed ....

<u>Mission Statement</u>

Visualise how you will look and feel when you have completed this goal, use as much detail as possible.

©Psycheuk.com2000

Use this graph to plot how you are doing throughout your Goalsetting

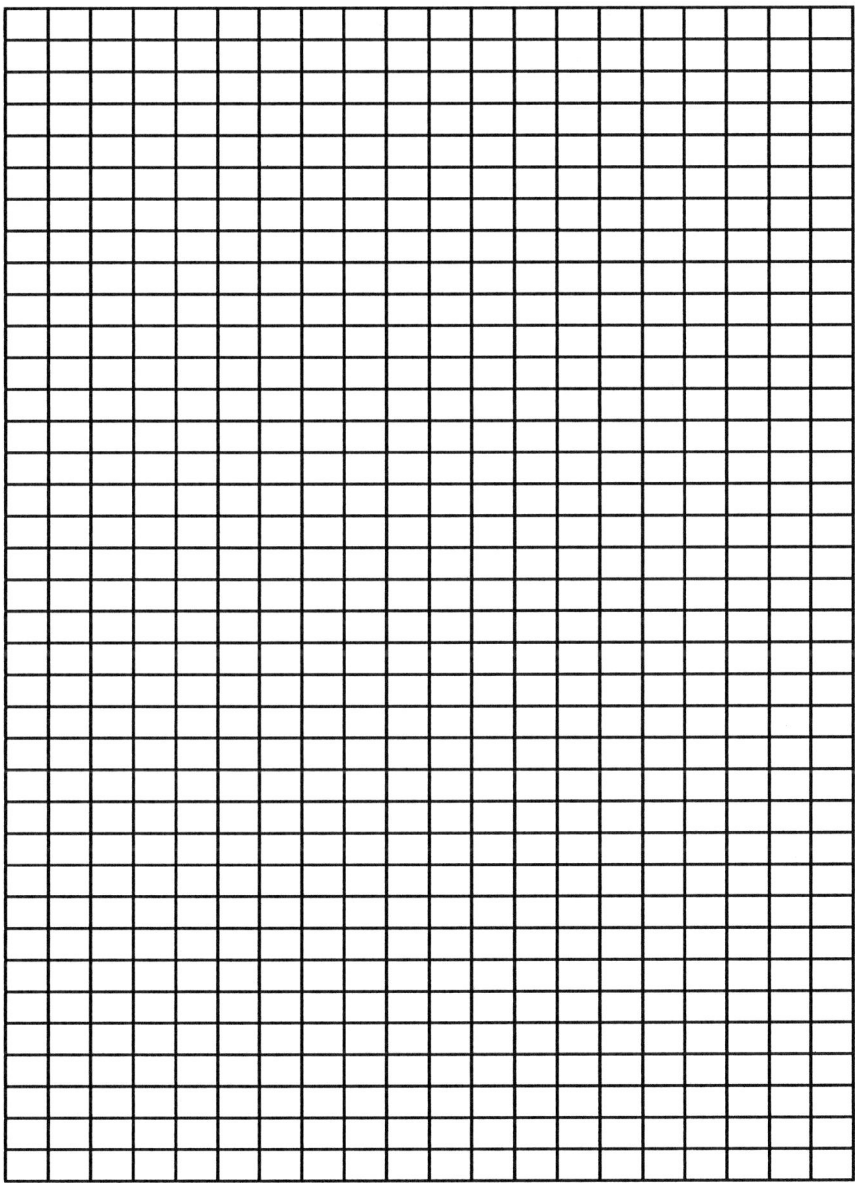

How do you spend your day – Appendix V

Time	Activity	Comments

Negative Feelings and Thoughts - Appendix VI

Situation	Thoughts	Feelings

About the Author

Andy Dowsett as well as being the Founder and Director of Psycheuk is also a qualified Counsellor and Hypnotherapist Practitioner. He performs applied research on techniques and strategies designed to teach us how to function as human beings and how to use that information to get the best out of ourselves. As Teacher, Consultant and Peak Performance Specialist, Andy assists people in breaking through the barriers of fear, limiting beliefs, procrastination and indecision.

Andy spent 9 Years in the Armed Forces travelling the world during the 80's and 90's, "psychologically a lot can be picked up when serving during world conflicts and along with my own dealings with these scenarios I have ventured into the world of learning the way a human acts and thinks under pressure!".

He has been playing tennis since a young age and has qualified within the Lawn Tennis Association as a CCA and within the Professional Tennis Registry as an Academy Professional Coach. In the year of our lord 2000 he was awarded the Prestigious USPTR Pro of the Year. As well as running Psycheuk he is the PTRuk National Tutor, teaching coaches throughout the UK, as well as lecturing at the yearly symposiums. He has also been found lecturing throughout Europe on his on-court psyche system.

Andy is available to lecture about the Tennis Psyche System at your seminar or club.

Printed in the United Kingdom
by Lightning Source UK Ltd.
118926UK00001B/160-363